The Royal Family

KING CHARLES III

IZZI HOWELL

WAYLAND

This updated paperback edition published in 2022
First published in Great Britain in 2018 by Hodder and Stoughton Limited
Copyright © Hodder and Stoughton Limited, 2018

ISBN 9781526306449

Wayland
An imprint of
Hachette Children's Group
Part of Hodder & Stoughton
Carmelite House
50 Victoria Embankment
London EC4Y 0DZ
An Hachette UK Company
www.hachette.co.uk
www.hachettechildrens.co.uk

Picture acknowledgements:
Alamy: Michael Dunlea 6; Getty Images: AFP 21; WPA Pool/Pool 17b; Jonathan Brady/WPA 7; Corbis 24;
Arthur Edwards/WPA 18, 26; Tim Graham 15t, 25t; Alastair Grant 22;WPA Pool/WPA 23t; Hulton Archive
5,14; Anwar Hussein/Wireimage 16; Samir Hussein/Wireimage front cover; Victoria Jones/AFP 4;
Keystone-France\Gamma-Rapho 8, 11; Dan Kitwood/Staff 23b; Popperfoto 9t, 12.
Shutterstock: Chameleon's Eye 17t, 30; Filipe Frazao 19; Frederic LeGrand-Comeo 27, 30;Lenscap
Photography 15c; Stephen Rees 20; Radomir Rezny 9b.
New Zealand Defence Force from Wellington, New Zealand:13.
Wikimedia Commons: Nbaba 10.
All graphic elements courtesy of Shutterstock.

CONTENTS

Who is King Charles? — 4

Royal power — 6

A prince is born — 8

Growing up — 10

A military man — 12

Marriage and children — 14

Charles' royal family — 16

Official duties — 18

Charities — 20

Working royals — 22

Hobbies and interests — 24

King Charles III — 26

Kings and queens of England — 28

The royal family tree — 29

Glossary — 30

Further information — 31

Index — 32

Who is King Charles?

King Charles III is King of the United Kingdom (UK). He came to the throne in 2022 after the death of his mother, Queen Elizabeth II. King Charles is supported in his work by his wife, Queen Consort Camilla, and other members of the royal family.

Head of State

King Charles is the UK's Head of State but it is the Prime Minister and other members of his government who run the country. He is also Head of the Commonwealth, a group of 54 countries around the world, many of which were once part of the British Empire. Some of these countries, including Australia, Canada and New Zealand, recognise him as Head of State.

On 10 September 2022, Charles was officially proclaimed King Charles III in an historic ceremony held at St James' Palace in London.

>

Heir apparent

In 1952, Prince Charles became heir to the throne when his grandfather, King George VI, died. He was only three years old at the time. His mother, Queen Elizabeth II, reigned for over seventy years until her death at the age of 96. This gave Prince Charles plenty of time to prepare for the role of king, longer than any other heir apparent in British history.

^
Members of the royal family, including Prince Charles and his sister, Princess Anne, on the balcony of Buckingham Palace after Queen Elizabeth II's coronation in 1953.

Prince of Wales

For most of his time as heir to the throne, he was known as the Prince of Wales. His son, Prince William, now takes the title of Prince of Wales. Charles had many other titles as well, including Earl of Chester, Duke of Cornwall, Duke of Edinburgh and Earl of Carrick. As a working royal, he represented the people of the UK at home and abroad, meeting people, opening important buildings, helping to build relationships between other countries and the UK and working for his charities.

DID YOU KNOW?

* Charles has visited over 100 different countries on royal duty, including Afghanistan, Brazil, Jamaica and Australia.

* Charles wrote and illustrated a children's book, The Old Man of Lochnagar.

* Charles enjoys painting landscapes with watercolour paints.

Royal power

In the past, kings and queens were very powerful. People believed that each monarch was chosen by God to rule over the country. Gradually, the royal family lost its power as new laws granted political power to members of the Houses of Parliament.

The King and his government

The UK is a democracy. This means that people of voting age in the UK vote for the politicians who they want to run the country. After an election, the leader of the winning political party visits the King to ask permission to form a government. The King is not allowed to refuse! Every week, the King meets with the Prime Minister in private.

The King and the armed forces

The King is Commander-in-Chief of the Armed Forces. Every new member of the British Army, the Royal Air Force and the Royal Marines swears an oath to serve him. In practice, he has no control over the armed forces as it is the government that decides how the armed forces are to be used.

< As Prince of Wales, Charles was Colonel-in-Chief of the Parachute Regiment and regularly visited them.

The royal coat of arms, the monarch's initials or the head of the monarch appear on many official documents, coins and bank notes, passports, postage stamps and even Royal Mail post boxes. As a new passport is issued in the name of His Majesty, the King does not need a passport to travel abroad. All other members of the royal family do need a passport.

∨ Charles and Camilla regularly meet with senior members of churches, including the Archbishop of Canterbury, the Most Reverend Justin Welby, shown here.

The King and the Church of England

The King has an important role to play as Supreme Governor of the Church of England. Church leaders swear an oath in which they promise to be loyal to the King. He appoints archbishops, bishops and the deans of cathedrals although it is leading members of the Church who decide on new appointments and pass on their choices through the Prime Minister. The King has a close relationship with the Church of Scotland although he is not its head. While following his own faith within the Church of England, the King celebrates harmony between all faiths in the UK and the Commonwealth.

A prince is born

On 14 November 1948, a prince was born at Buckingham Palace. A message posted on the railings of the palace announced the birth of Charles to the world.

Early life

Charles was the first child of Prince Philip and Princess Elizabeth. In 1950, his sister Anne was born. Even before their mother became queen in 1952, she often had to spend time away from her children performing royal duties or spending time with their father, who was working for the Royal Navy in Malta. After she became queen, she was even busier so Charles and Anne were often looked after by nannies and by their grandmother, Queen Elizabeth the Queen Mother.

In 1953, Charles attended his mother's coronation at the age of four, along with his younger sister Anne. Charles' grandmother stands on the right of the Queen in this photo. >

Off to school

Charles was taught by a governess at the palace until he was eight years old. Then, Elizabeth and Philip decided he should go to school. Charles went to private school in London for ten months. Then, his parents sent him to a boarding school called Cheam, in Hampshire, in 1957. Charles lived, studied and spent most of his free time at school away from his family. However, he could spend holidays with his family at royal homes in Scotland and Norfolk.

Eight-year-old Charles (centre) and his classmates walk through the streets of London on a school trip. >

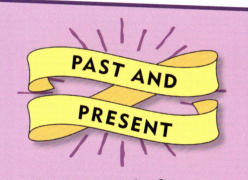

PAST AND PRESENT

Charles was the first ever heir apparent to go to school. In the past, royal children, including Queen Elizabeth II, were taught by private tutors at home. Today, most royal children go to school.

Full board

At boarding school, Charles had to follow a strict routine. He had to wake up at 7.15 a.m., say prayers at 7.45 a.m. and eat breakfast at 8 a.m., before lessons started at 9. When he wasn't in class, Charles played sports, such as cricket. He also enjoyed acting in plays. While Charles was at Cheam, his mother announced that Charles was going to be given the title Prince of Wales.

Prince Charles spent some of his holidays at Sandringham House in Norfolk. >

Growing up

• • •

Like many members of the royal family, Charles spent his teenage years at boarding school. His royal duties would have to wait until he had finished his education.

Prince Philip had a pilot's licence. He flew the plane that took Charles up to Scotland before his first day at Gordonstoun.

A new school

At the age of 13, Charles started at a new school, Gordonstoun, in the north east of Scotland. Charles' father, Prince Philip, had gone to the same school. The teachers at Gordonstoun were very strict. Charles was not always happy there. Despite this, Charles thinks the school developed his willpower and determination, while encouraging his love of the outdoors, acting, music and archaeology.

∨ Gordonstoun School

New challenges

In 1966, Charles spent two terms as an exchange student in Australia. He enjoyed his time abroad, going on cross-country expeditions in the heat and spotting snakes, leeches and venomous spiders. When he came back to Gordonstoun, he was made head boy. He had more responsibility and tried to help the other students. Before he left the school, he took A Level exams and received a grade B in History and a C in French.

University life

In 1967, Charles went to the University of Cambridge to study archaeology and anthropology. Later, he changed subject and studied history instead. He graduated in 1970 with a 2:2 degree. This was the first time that an heir apparent had graduated from university. While he was at university, Charles spent a term at the University of Aberystwyth, learning Welsh for his role as the Prince of Wales. In his final year of university, he started going to events and representing the royal family when he wasn't in lessons.

∨ Charles enjoyed taking part in drama productions with other students at the University of Cambridge.

A military man

Like his father, grandfather and many other relatives, Charles had a military career. He spent over five years in active service in the Royal Navy in the 1970s. He is now Commander-in-Chief of the Armed Forces (see page 6).

The Royal Air Force

Charles began serving in the Royal Air Force in March 1971. He already had a pilot's licence, so he flew himself to the training centre by plane. He trained as a jet pilot and was awarded his RAF Wings in August 1971.

∧ Charles had to take many flying lessons while training in the RAF.

At sea

In September 1971, Charles joined the Royal Navy. He trained at the Royal Naval College in Dartmouth, where his father and great uncle had also trained. He served on different ships and learned how to organise and lead a ship full of sailors.

He never fought in a war but he learned skills that a sailor would need in battle, such as escaping from a submarine. Charles also qualified as a helicopter pilot. For the final ten months of his service in 1976, he was given command of his own ship. He was in charge of HMS *Bronington*, a ship that was used to look for and destroy dangerous mines at sea.

MILITARY ROYALS

There is a long history of the royal family serving in the armed forces. During the Second World War, Queen Elizabeth was the first royal woman to join the army, where she trained as a mechanic. Charles' sons William and Harry both trained in the military. William worked as a search and rescue pilot in the Royal Air Force, while Harry was in the army for 10 years and was posted to the front line of conflicts.

Support for the armed services

Charles left active service in the armed forces in 1976. As Prince of Wales, he held many honorary titles, such as Admiral of the Fleet, Field Marshal and Marshal of the Royal Air Force. He supported and continues to support members of the armed forces in many ways, including visiting injured soldiers in hospital and acting as patron for charities that support members of the armed forces and their families.

Charles meets soldiers on a trip to an army training centre.
∨

Members of the royal family send gifts and personal messages to soldiers serving abroad.

Marriage and children

Charles' personal life has not always been easy. However, his two children, William and Harry, have always brought him happiness and pride.

Finding a wife

In his early twenties, Charles fell in love with Camilla Shand but she went on to marry someone else. In 1980, Charles started a relationship with Lady Diana Spencer. In February 1981, Charles and Diana became engaged. They married five months later in July 1981. Their wedding was a huge event around the world. Some people said it was 'the wedding of the century'.

∨ **Charles and Diana leave St Paul's Cathedral, London, after their wedding.**

7.62 metres — the length of Diana's wedding dress train.

10,000 — the number of sequins and pearls on Diana's dress.

600,000 — the number of people who watched from the streets of London.

750 million — the number of people who watched on TV around the world.

Becoming a family

Charles' and Diana's first child, William, was born on 21 June 1982. Charles was with Diana at William's birth. It was the first time a royal father had been at the birth of his child. Their second child, Henry (Harry), was born on 15 September 1984. The boys came with Charles and Diana on some royal visits.

Charles with William and Harry in 1985 >

Difficult times

Charles and Diana did not always have a happy relationship. They separated in 1992 and got divorced in 1996. Diana was killed in a car crash in Paris in 1997. She was 36 years old. The royal family and many people around the world were shocked and upset. Over a million people took to the streets of London to watch the funeral procession and service, while over two billion watched around the world on TV.

The Mail ON SUNDAY

FAREWELL: The coffin of the Princess of Wales leaving Westminster Abbey yesterday
THE DAY WE ALL SAID GOODBYE

< Newspapers showed the story of Diana's funeral. Charles, William and Harry walked behind the coffin on the way to the church for the funeral service.

Moving on

After Diana's death, Charles focused on his sons. He helped them to cope with their loss. After the funeral, he kept them away from the public eye while they grieved. Several years later, in 2005, Charles remarried. His second wife is Camilla, the woman he first fell in love with in the early 1970s. The princes attended Charles and Camilla's wedding and have developed an excellent relationship with their stepmother.

ROYAL TALK

'She's a wonderful woman, and she's made our father very, very happy, which is the most important thing. William and I love her to bits.'

Prince Harry spoke in an interview about Camilla in 2005.

15

Charles' royal family

Charles has two sons, William and Harry. Together with Charles' wife Camilla and his five grandchildren, they make up part of the British royal family.

Children

Charles had two sons, Prince William and Prince Henry (Harry). William married Kate Middleton in 2011. After their wedding, the Queen gave them the titles of the Duke and Duchess of Cambridge, but since the Queen's death in 2022, they are now known as the Prince and Princess of Wales. Harry married Meghan Markle in 2018. They were given the titles the Duke and Duchess of Sussex.

∨ Meghan, Harry, William and Kate watch a fly-past of RAF planes from the balcony of Buckingham Palace in 2018.

Meghan ↓   Harry ↓   William →   Kate ↓

ROYAL TALK

'Grandparenthood is a unique moment in anyone's life ... so I am enormously proud and happy to be a grandfather for the first time.'

Charles spoke about the birth of his first grandchild, George, in 2013.

V Charles and Camilla at their wedding in 2005.

Grandchildren

William and Kate have three children, and Harry and Meghan have two children so now Charles is a grandfather too. Charles loves reading stories to his grandchildren and does funny voices for all of the characters!

V Harry and Meghan on their wedding day in 2018.

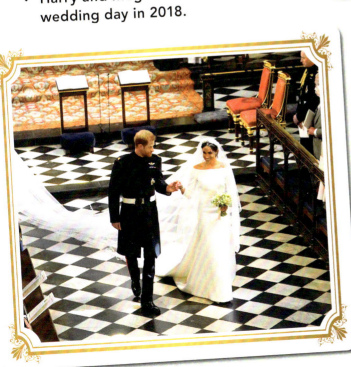

STEPPING BACK

In 2020, Harry and Meghan announced that they were stepping back from their role as senior members of the royal family. It was a difficult decision as it meant that they would no longer carry out royal duties. They moved to the United States to start a new life with their young family.

Official duties

The King has hundreds of official duties every year, both in the UK and abroad. He is always in the public eye and rarely gets time in private.

∧ In 2022, Charles read out the Queen's Speech at the State Opening of Parliament.

Royal ceremonies

The King attends the State Opening of Parliament at the start of each parliamentary year. In a ceremony dating back hundreds of years, he travels to the House of Commons with his crown and other symbols of royal authority before reading out the King's Speech. The speech is written by the government, not the King. In November, the King leads the nation in mourning the dead of two world wars and other conflicts at the Remembrance Sunday service at the Cenotaph in London.

Investitures

King Charles and other members of the royal family present people with their awards at ceremonies called investitures. People are awarded an honour, such as an OBE, MBE or knighthood, for their outstanding achievements, service to others or for bravery. The royals congratulate each person individually as they present them with a medal.

State visits, banquets and tours

The UK government relies on the royal family to strengthen relationships between them and foreign leaders through state visits and royal tours. During a state visit, the visitors are invited to attend various events including a grand state banquet, usually held at the King's royal home, Buckingham Palace. As Prince of Wales, Charles often travelled abroad on royal tours and continues to do so. He meets foreign leaders and diplomats as well as the general public. He also welcomes heads of state or other important people to one of his homes for an audience, a royal meeting, if they are visiting the UK on business.

Charles meets the public on a visit to New Zealand when he was still Prince of Wales. ∨

Charities

●○●

Members of the royal family are patron or president of over 3,000 different charities. Charles has been the president of a group of charities that raise over £100 million every year. This money is used to help people and projects in need, both in the UK and abroad.

The Prince's Trust

After leaving the Royal Navy, Charles wanted to help the lives of disadvantaged young people in the UK. He set up the Prince's Trust in 1976, a charity that helps young people to get into work, education or training. The charity is still going and helps thousands of young people every year.

∨ Charles prepares food with people who attend a Prince's Trust workshop that teaches them cookery skills.

ROYAL TALK

'You can see how it is possible to turn young people's lives around and give them self-confidence, self-worth and self-esteem.'

Charles spoke about the importance of the Prince's Trust.

The Prince's Trust has helped over a million people since it was founded in 1976.

∧
The British Asian Trust helps girls in South Asia to attend school for long enough to get a good education.

Helping other countries

The Prince's Charities also help to transform lives abroad. One of the charities in the group is the British Asian Trust, which invests in education, healthcare and employment in South Asia. This helps to improve people's lives in the long run, rather than just giving money as a short-term solution. So far, it has helped over six million people.

Camilla's work

Queen Consort Camilla is patron or president of over 90 charities focusing on issues such as literacy, poverty, homelessness and animal welfare. She is passionate about the importance of young people developing a love of reading. She has also raised awareness of the disease osteoporosis, which weakens bones, and organises a fundraising walk every year in Scotland to raise money for sufferers.

Working royals

Working members of the royal family carry out thousands of official duties at home and abroad every year. They include Prince William and Princess Kate, Princess Anne, Prince Edward, Countess Sophie, the Duke and Duchess of Gloucester and the Duke of Kent.

William, Prince of Wales

As Charles' eldest son, Prince William is heir to the throne. He attends official engagements alongside Charles or represents his father if he is unable to attend. He is a very busy working royal. Even before he became Prince of Wales, he had visited several countries on royal tours, alongside his wife. He attends numerous charity events and is very involved with the work of the Royal Foundation, especially its work aimed at improving the lives of young people, saving wildlife and combatting climate change.

Recognising the need to take urgent action to protect wildlife and combat climate change, William and the Royal Foundation launched the Earthshot Prize in 2020, to seek out and fund the best ideas to fix the planet.

Princess of Wales

Kate, the Princess of Wales, is another busy working royal. She carries out many official duties and devotes a huge amount of time to supporting charities and organisations. Working with the Royal Foundation, she brings attention to the importance of improving the lives of young children and their parents as well as supporting people to improve their mental health.

Princess Anne

Officially known as the Princess Royal, Princess Anne, the King's sister, supports him with advice and represents the royal family at hundreds of official events every year. In addition, she is involved with over 300 charities large and small, including Save the Children.

∧
Kate and William meet a therapy puppy, Alfie, who will be used to help support the wellbeing of staff and patients at a community hospital.

Prince Edward and Countess Sophie

Prince Edward, Earl of Wessex, is a full-time working royal, often supported by his wife, Sophie, Countess of Wessex. As well as carrying out official duties, they both attend a huge number of charity events and are closely involved with their own charities, including the Earl and Countess of Wessex Trust. Prince Edward is especially supportive of organisations that provide opportunities to young people.

< Prince Edward and Countess Sophie are given a tour of the Chelsea Flower Show in 2022, which has a theme of calm and mindfulness.

Hobbies and interests

As well as his serious commitment to conservation and combatting climate change, Charles has a wide range of different hobbies and interests.

Performing arts

Ever since he was a child, Charles has enjoyed theatre and music. While at school, he acted in plays and played the cello and the trumpet. As Prince of Wales, he worked with many charities to help children experience the arts. He also enjoys attending theatrical and musical performances.

∧ Charles meets the cast of the musical *Wicked* in London.

Charles

Harry

William

∧ Charles, William and Harry take part in a charity polo match in 2005.

Polo

At the age of 15, Charles played his first game of polo. He immediately fell in love with the game and took part in matches all around the world. He also introduced William and Harry to the game and they remain keen players. Charles took part in many fund-raising charity matches over the years but stopped playing in 2005. He still enjoys watching the sport.

During a polo match, Charles was hit in the throat and lost his voice for 10 days!

Gardening and plants

Charles loves spending time outdoors in nature. He helped plan and plant up the organic garden at his country home, Highgrove House, in Gloucestershire. As well as a wildflower meadow, bushes clipped into interesting shapes and a big vegetable plot, the garden is full of colour and scent from flowering plants.

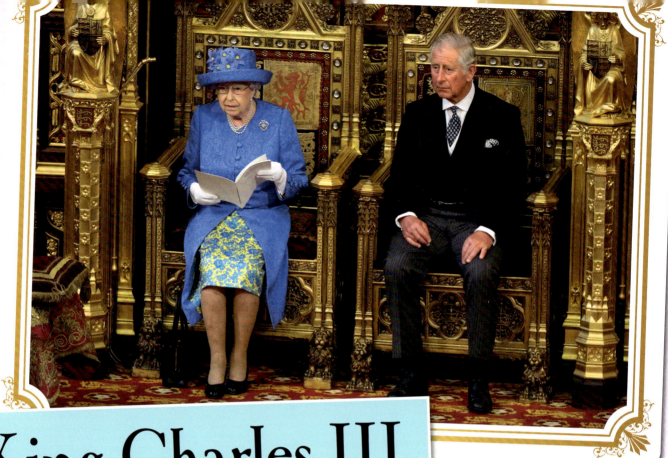

King Charles III

As Queen Elizabeth II grew older, she gradually asked Charles to take over some of her duties. When she died on 8 September 2022, he immediately became King Charles III.

∧

Charles joined his mother, Queen Elizabeth II, at the State Opening of Parliament in 2017.

The Queen's legacy

During his speech to the nation the day after the Queen's death, Charles made the same promise as his mother had made as a young woman, a promise of lifelong service to the people of the UK and the Commonwealth.

WHAT'S IN A NAME?

Some kings and queens change their name when they start their reign. Charles' grandfather, King George VI, was called Albert before he became king. Charles could have used any of his four names, Charles Philip Arthur or George, but decided to stick with Charles III.

Private v public

King Charles has to keep his opinions to himself. In private, he continues to support the causes close to his heart. Because of his working life as a monarch, he is often seen on TV and in newspapers. At the same time, he continues to value his private life and tries to protect the private lives of his children and grandchildren. He hopes that his life of public duty will continue to show the value of the British royal family to the wider public.

Heir to the throne

William, Prince of Wales, will one day inherit the throne from his father. He has been preparing for this role by watching and learning from his grandmother, Queen Elizabeth II, and will continue to learn from his father, King Charles III.

< Prince William is heir apparent.

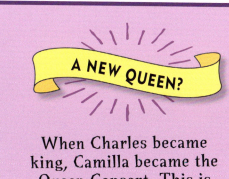

A NEW QUEEN?

When Charles became king, Camilla became the Queen Consort. This is the title for the wife of a monarch.

Kings and Queens of England

The House of Normandy

William I *(William the Conqueror)*	1066–1087
William II *(William Rufus)*	1087–1100
Henry I	1100–1135
Stephen	1135–1154

The House of Plantagenet

Henry II	1154–1189
Richard I *(Richard the Lionheart)*	1189–1199
John	1199–1216
Henry III	1216–1272
Edward I	1272–1307
Edward II	1307–1327
Edward III	1327–1377
Richard II	1377–1399

The House of Lancaster

Henry IV	1399–1413
Henry V	1413–1422
Henry VI	1422–1461

The House of York

Edward IV	1461–1483
Edward V	1483–1483
Richard III	1483–1485

The House of Tudor

Henry VII	1485–1509
Henry VIII	1509–1547
Edward VI	1547–1553
Jane	1553–1553
Mary I	1553–1558
Elizabeth I	1558–1603

The House of Stuart

James I (James VI of Scotland)	1603–1625
Charles I	1625–1649
Commonwealth declared	
Oliver Cromwell Lord Protector	1653–1658
Richard Cromwell Lord Protector	1658–1659
Monarchy restored	
Charles II	1649 *(restored 1660)*–1685
James II *(James VII of Scotland)*	1685–1688
William III and Mary II	1689–1694 (Mary)
	1702 *(William)*
Anne	1702–1714

The House of Hanover

George I	1714–1727
George II	1727–1760
George III	1760–1820
George IV	1820–1830
William IV	1830–1837
Victoria	1837–1901

The House of Saxe-Coburg – becomes House of Windsor in 1917

Edward VII	1901–1910
George V	1910–1936
Edward VIII *(abdicated)*	1936–1936
George VI	1936–1952
Elizabeth II	1952–2022
Charles III	2022–

The royal family tree

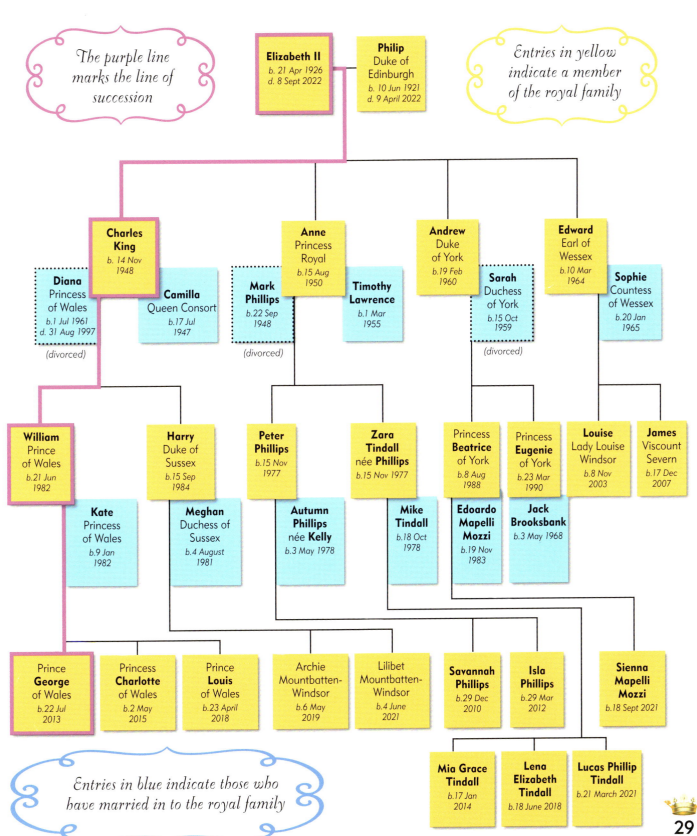

The purple line marks the line of succession

Entries in yellow indicate a member of the royal family

Elizabeth II
b. 21 Apr 1926
d. 8 Sept 2022

Philip
Duke of Edinburgh
b. 10 Jun 1921
d. 9 April 2022

Charles
King
b. 14 Nov 1948

Diana
Princess of Wales
b.1 Jul 1961
d. 31 Aug 1997
(divorced)

Camilla
Queen Consort
b.17 Jul 1947

Anne
Princess Royal
b.15 Aug 1950

Mark Phillips
b.22 Sep 1948
(divorced)

Timothy Lawrence
b.1 Mar 1955

Andrew
Duke of York
b.19 Feb 1960

Sarah
Duchess of York
b.15 Oct 1959
(divorced)

Edward
Earl of Wessex
b.10 Mar 1964

Sophie
Countess of Wessex
b.20 Jan 1965

William
Prince of Wales
b.21 Jun 1982

Kate
Princess of Wales
b.9 Jan 1982

Harry
Duke of Sussex
b.15 Sep 1984

Meghan
Duchess of Sussex
b.4 August 1981

Peter Phillips
b.15 Nov 1977

Autumn Phillips
née **Kelly**
b.3 May 1978

Zara Tindall
née **Phillips**
b.15 Nov 1977

Mike Tindall
b.18 Oct 1978

Princess Beatrice
of York
b.8 Aug 1988

Edoardo Mapelli Mozzi
b.19 Nov 1983

Princess Eugenie
of York
b.23 Mar 1990

Jack Brooksbank
b.3 May 1968

Louise
Lady Louise Windsor
b.8 Nov 2003

James
Viscount Severn
b.17 Dec 2007

Prince **George** of Wales
b.22 Jul 2013

Princess **Charlotte** of Wales
b.2 May 2015

Prince **Louis** of Wales
b.23 April 2018

Archie Mountbatten-Windsor
b.6 May 2019

Lilibet Mountbatten-Windsor
b.4 June 2021

Savannah Phillips
b.29 Dec 2010

Isla Phillips
b.29 Mar 2012

Sienna Mapelli Mozzi
b.18 Sept 2021

Mia Grace Tindall
b.17 Jan 2014

Lena Elizabeth Tindall
b.18 June 2018

Lucas Phillip Tindall
b.21 March 2021

Entries in blue indicate those who have married in to the royal family

Glossary

abdicate when the heir to the throne steps down and refuses the position

coat of arms a symbol that is used by a royal family or a monarch

Commonwealth, the a group of countries, including the UK, that were previously part of the British Empire and share trade agreements

consort the husband or wife of the monarch

coronation the ceremony at which someone is made the king or queen

diplomat someone whose job is to live in another country and keep a good relationship between their government and that country's government

governess a woman employed to teach children in the family's home

graduate to complete a degree at university or other course

heir apparent the first person in line to the throne

maternal a maternal grandparent is one of the parents of your mother

monarch a king or queen

noble describes someone from a high-ranking family, who may have titles and own land

patron a person who supports an organisation or charity

polo a sport played on horseback in which players hit a ball with long wooden hammers

Prime Minister the person in charge of a government

represent to act on behalf of someone or many people. Prince Charles represents the UK when he attends events and meetings with leaders from other countries

United Kingdom (UK) a country made up of England, Scotland, Wales and Northern Ireland

Further information

Places to see:

Buckingham Palace,
London SW1A 1AA
Open to the public most summers
www.rct.uk/visit/buckingham-palace

Holyroodhouse
Edinburgh EH8 8DX
The King's official residence in Scotland
and home of Scottish royal history
www.rct.uk/visit/palace-of-holyroodhouse

Windsor Castle
Windsor, Berkshire SL4 1NJ
Open to the public throughout most of
the year. Check website for opening days
and times.
www.rct.uk/visit/buckingham-palace

Websites to visit:

The official website of the royal family has
details of all its members, as well as royal
residences and events such as Trooping
the Colour:
www.royal.uk/royal-family

Visit the website of The Prince's Trust
to find out more about the work that
they do to help young people:
www.princes-trust.org.uk

Books to read:

A Royal Childhood: 200 Years of Royal
Babies
by Liz Gogerly, Franklin Watts, 2017

The Story of Britain
by Mike Manning and Brita Granström,
Franklin Watts, 2016

Queen Elizabeth II's Britain
by Jacqui Bailey, Franklin Watts, 2015

Index

Anne, Princess 8, 22, 23
Australia 4, 5, 11

birth 8
Buckingham Palace 19, 31
British Asian Trust 21

Camilla, the Queen Consort 5, 7, 14, 15, 16, 17, 21, 27
charities 20–21, 22, 23
Cheam School 9
childhood 8–9, 10–11
Church of England 7
Commonwealth 4, 7, 26
coronation 5, 8

Diana, Princess of Wales 14, 15
divorce 15

Earthshot Prize 22
Edward, Prince 22, 23
Elizabeth II, Queen 4, 5, 8, 9, 26
Elizabeth, the Queen Mother 8

gardening 25
George VI, King 5
George, Prince 17, 29
Gordonstoun School 10, 11
government 6

Harry, Prince 13, 14, 15, 16, 17
heir apparent 5, 27
Highgrove House 25

investitures 19

Kate, Duchess of Cambridge 16, 17, 22, 23
Kings and Queens of England 28

Meghan, Duchess of Sussex 16, 17
military 6, 12–13

New Zealand 4, 19

passport 7
performing arts 11, 24
Philip, Prince 8, 29
polo 25
postboxes 7
Prince's Trust, the 20

Remembrance Sunday 18
royal family tree 29
Royal Foundation 22, 23

Sandringham 9
Sophie, Countess of Wessex 22, 23
State Opening of Parliament 18, 26
state visits 19

University of Cambridge 11

weddings 14, 15, 16, 17
William, Prince 5, 13, 14, 15, 16, 17, 22, 23, 27